MW00388833

To the Maslin Family

:)

The Adventures of

Tooth Fairy Tommy

Written by: Stefanie Hilarczyk

Illustrations by: Taylor Coon

In Tooth Fairy Kingdom, a land not too far away, lived two rather sparkly and silly tooth fairies - Tooth Tommy and Tooth Tina - who were brother and sister.

They were not too alike or too different. **TOMMY** and **TINA** might have been tiny in size but nothing they did was tiny at all - especially when new tooth fairy Tommy was anywhere around.

He was smaller than the rest of the fairies, and his little pointy ears didn't match his really big feet.

Tommy's wings were too small, making it all the harder for him to keep up with his sister and the other fairies.

He was always so forgetful and getting into trouble-nothing like his sister, **TOOTH TINA**. She was older and wiser. She had been a tooth fairy for a long time. Tommy was only a tooth fairy in training.

He was always running late and making kids worry that their teeth would not be taken by their tooth fairy and no money or prizes would be left for them in place for their teeth.

Tommy was so horrible at his job that kids were constantly trying to trap him and catch him taking their teeth! One time, he was running so late he forgot to take the child's tooth!

Then one day, Tommy was given a chance of a lifetime! He was told by **TOOTH FAIRY HEADMASTER BOB** that there was a special tooth assignment that he must take care of all by himself! This would be Tommy's last chance to get the job right! There was a little boy named Jimmy who had just lost his very first tooth!

Tommy was SO excited! He had never visited a child who lost their first tooth! Tommy happily traveled with his little wings and big feet through the **LAZY TOOTH RIVER,**

and then up the **DECAY MOUNTAINS** and through the **FLOSSY GRASSY** paths, until he got to Jimmy's house.

He stopped at Jimmy's window, where he sprinkled his magic tooth fairy dust and joyfully flew into Jimmy's room. To his surprise, he was on time! There Jimmy lay sound asleep in his bed.

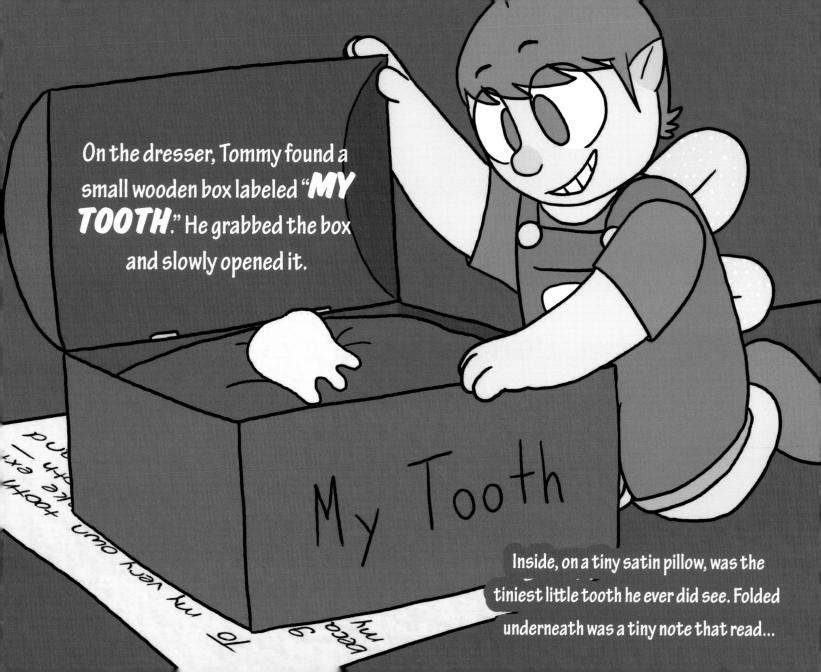

To my very own tooth fairy,
Please take extra
good care of my tooth —
because it came from me and
my mouth!

Signed,
Jimmy

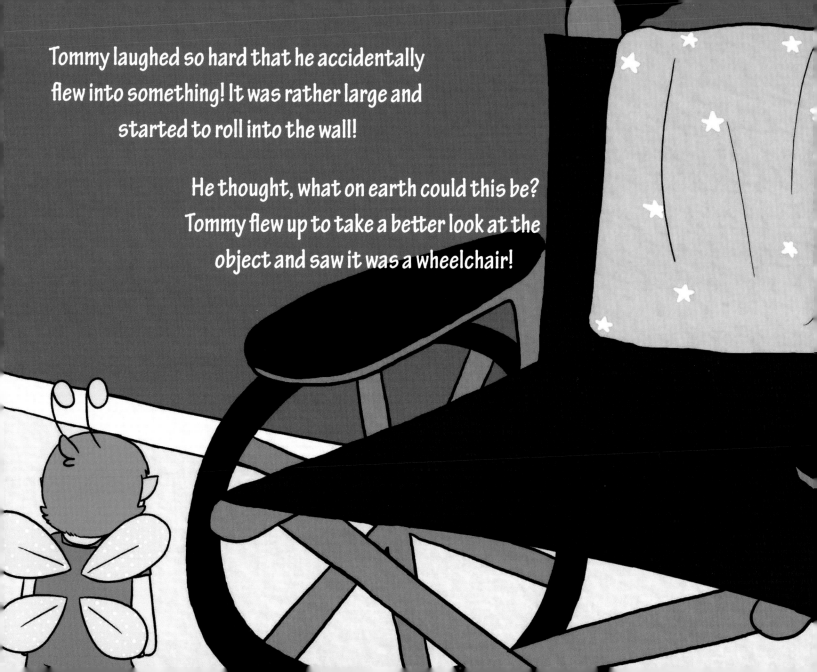

Tommy laughed so hard that he accidentally flew into something! It was rather large and started to roll into the wall!

He thought, what on earth could this be? Tommy flew up to take a better look at the object and saw it was a wheelchair!

He turned to look at Jimmy sleeping so soundly and
then noticed sticking out from the cowboy print
sheets, leg braces on Jimmy's tiny little legs.

Tommy was confused. Why would a little guy like Jimmy
need leg braces? Why would he need a wheelchair?
Tommy quickly started writing a note back to Jimmy.

Dear Jimmy,
   I'm your very own tooth fairy. This is my first week on the job! I was so shocked to find out this was your first tooth! You're one special kid! I think we have a lot in common! I'm so excited we're having this toothy adventure together!

                    your friend,
                  Tooth Tommy

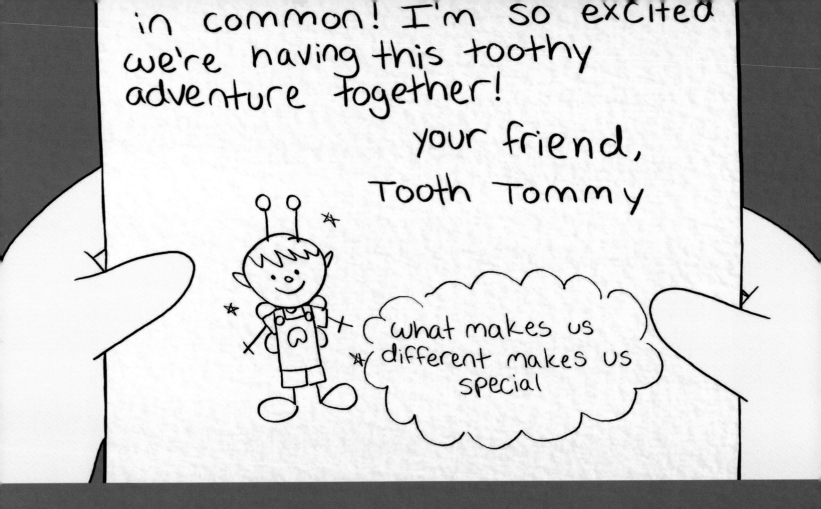

At the bottom of the page, Tommy drew a portrait of himself-
with his tiny legs, big feet, little wings and not so perfect ears.
Next to the picture, in tiny letters, he added, "What makes
us different makes us special."

When Tommy was all done, he flew back to the window to spread his magic dust. Then suddenly he turned around because he had almost forgotten to take the tiny little tooth. Tommy smiled back at Jimmy and flew out the window.

On the way back to Tooth Fairy Kingdom, Tommy began to wonder about Jimmy. He thought about his wheelchair and his tiny little leg braces. Tommy wondered what it would be like if he needed leg braces too!

He wondered who pushed Jimmy in his wheelchair or if Jimmy could move himself around in it. Tommy began to feel something deep inside his fairy spirit.

When Tommy finally arrived home, he ran straight to Headmaster Bob to tell him all about Jimmy and to ask him about the feeling he was feeling. He wasn't feeling too happy or too sad.

And he wasn't feeling too alone or too different anymore. He was feeling all new things - caring, kindness, togetherness, warmth, understanding, and joy. He wondered what all these feelings meant.

HEADMASTER

BRUSH YOUR TEETH!

Empathy is different from sympathy. Do you know what **SYMPATHY** means? That's feeling sorrow for someone's misfortune or sadness. It's different from empathy. "I gave you Jimmy, so you can see all the wonders of different people - and to show you we really aren't alone and that being different isn't bad" said Headmaster Bob.

"When you have empathy you really feel magic. That's when you feel you need to help someone even if that person can't do anything to help you back. And helping makes you feel happy."

As Headmaster Bob continued to talk, Tommy's wings began to sparkle and move.

The most beautiful orange color appeared, and his wings began to fly so high that he began to cry the happiest of tears.

Headmaster Bob told Tommy that we all must be kind and gentle, and understanding towards everyone. We all must have empathy. When we do, great things happen!

kind, gentle, understanding

When Tommy had taken the time to write back to Jimmy, He showed caring and kindness!

Each tooth fairy must possess special traits before they officially become a tooth fairy.

EMPATHY

That's exactly what happened to Tooth Fairy Tommy! Tommy visited Jimmy for each new lost tooth. They wrote notes to each other on each visit.

ABOUT THE AUTHOR:

Stefanie Hilarczyk is a graduate of the Institute of Children's Literature. She is a special needs advocate, writer and speaker. She can be found at the beach near her home and finding cool things to do with her family near the shore. She resides in New Jersey with her two children and awesome husband for 16 years. You can find her on Instagram @Stef_Hil. She would like to dedicate this book to her amazing children! And, a special thank you to Taylor whom she only met this year and agreed to give her talents for the artwork of this book!